WELCOME TO THE WORLD OF

Orangutans

Diane Swanson

WALRUS
B O O K S

Edited by Elizabeth McLean
Cover design by Steve Penner
Interior design by Margaret Ng
Typeset by Marjolein Visser
Photo credits: Anup Shah/Dembinsky Photo Associates iv, 2, 4, 6, 10, 12, 14, 18, 20, 22, 24; Darrell Gulin/Dembinsky Photo Associates 8, 16; Daniel J. Cox / Natural Exposures 26

Printed and bound in Canada

Library and Archives Canada Cataloguing in Publication
Swanson, Diane, 1944–
    Welcome to the world of orangutans / Diane Swanson.
    Includes index.
    ISBN 1-55285-472-8
    1. Orangutan—Juvenile literature. I. Title.
    QL737.P96S83 2004   j599.88′3   C2004-904188-6

For more information on this series and other Whitecap titles, visit our web site at www.whitecap.ca.

Learn more about orangutans and help them survive by joining the
Orangutan Foundation International. Contact:

Orangutan Foundation International
4201 Wilshire Blvd., Suite 407
Los Angeles, CA 90010
Phone: 323-938-6046
Fax: 323-938-6047
Website: www.orangutan.org

The publisher acknowledges the support of the Canada Council for the Arts and the Cultural Services Branch of the Government of British Columbia for our publishing program. We acknowledge the financial support of the Government of Canada through the Book Industry Development Program for our publishing activities.

Contents

World of Difference

An orangutan doesn't need a tail. Long limbs help it travel easily through the woods.

ORANGUTANS ARE NO MONKEYS. They're great apes—along with gorillas and chimpanzees. Like all great apes, orangutans (oh-RANG-uh-tans) have long, muscular arms, and strong hands and feet. But they don't have any tails.

These great apes are big beasts. Males can weigh more than 90 kilograms (200 pounds) and stand up to 1.5 metres (5 feet) tall. Females are much shorter and about half as heavy. Of all the animals that live in trees, orangutans are the biggest.

Orangutans have large brains, too. They can think, learn, and remember. When

they're picking fruit in trees, they form handles by bunching vines together, then they hang onto them. Orangutans also make fly swatters from branches and backscratchers from sticks. Sometimes, they use sticks as spoons to scoop out seeds inside fruits. And to keep cool and dry when they're resting, they make covers out of leaves.

Mighty jaws and teeth make crunching a snap for an orangutan!

Most orangutans learn to do things by imitating other orangutans. Some learn by watching people in camps. There they've discovered how to dig with shovels, sweep with brooms, open locks, untie knots, scribble in books, and comb their hair.

Captured orangutans have even learned to communicate with people. At one zoo, they pointed to different symbols to get what they wanted. A rectangle with a line through it stood for "banana," and a dot in a circle meant "cup."

OUTSTANDING ORANGUTANS

Orangutans are amazing in many ways:

- The huge jaws of orangutans can crush the tough shells of coconuts.
- Male orangutans are about seven times stronger than male human beings.
- To keep dry, orangutans might wear rain hats made of leaves.
- Orangutans use twigs to remove insects from cracks or holes in trees.

Where in the World

High in a
bamboo forest,
an orangutan
looks down
at its world.

PEOPLE OF THE FOREST. That's what
"orangutans" means. After all, orangutans
resemble people and live in a forest—the
jungles of Borneo and Sumatra in Southeast
Asia. Orangutans are the only great apes
found in the wild outside of Africa.

Most orangutans do all their eating,
sleeping, traveling, mating, and playing
in the trees. They can climb as high as
45 metres (150 feet), and they might not
touch the ground for three weeks at a time.

Orangutans are well built for the
treetop life. Their arms are long enough to
reach easily from branch to branch. Their

5

Time for bed. Two orangutans settle in their nest for the night.

hooklike hands and feet are made for climbing. And their hips allow their legs to swing freely, helping the apes move between trees.

Even the color of orangutans is best for jungle living. As sunlight filters through the dense growth, it bounces off the leaves, reflecting green colors but absorbing reddish shades. Because many orangutans have reddish-brown hair, the light helps them disappear from sight.

For most of the time, a male orangutan travels his world alone. If he meets a female willing to be his mate, he stays with her for a few days, then heads off on his own again.

A female orangutan normally lives only with her young ones. But when the jungle trees are heavy with fruit, small groups gather, sharing the company as well as the wonderful feast.

The orangutan is a sleepy ape. It gets up and goes to bed with the sun. In between, it might flop down on a tree branch or a tough vine to snatch a nap or two.

Every night, an orangutan builds a new sleeping nest in a tree by weaving several leafy branches together. It might also make a pillow of twigs. The orangutan usually beds down close to where it ate dinner—and where there will be food the next morning.

7

World Full of Food

EATING CAN TAKE HALF AN ORANGUTAN'S DAY. In a few hours, the ape can devour all the fruit from a single tree, then move on to find more.

Orangutans eat a wide variety of fruits, but they have to work hard to get all they want. The trees they visit usually grow far apart, and the fruits ripen at different times. Some fruit trees produce a good crop only once every four to seven years.

That keeps the orangutans traveling— and using their heads. They have to remember where to find certain trees and when to visit them. Scientists think that

Finding no fruit to eat, an orangutan lunches on leaves and stems.

9

Some orangutans pluck leaves to clean off food that sticks to their mouths.

the orangutans keep mental "maps" of the jungle in mind so they don't waste time and energy searching for food that's not there.

Luckily, an orangutan stores energy as body fat whenever fruit is plentiful. It can also fill up on foods that are usually handy—stems, leaves, flowers, seeds, nuts, honey, fungi, and a range of insects. Now and then, the orangutan might catch and eat a small mammal, such as the monkeylike slow loris. And eating a bit of clay weakens any toxin, or poison, in the food.

Many orangutans use tools when they eat. Some pad their hands with leaves to protect their fingers from sharp spines that grow on certain fruits. In parts of the jungle, orangutans use leaves like napkins, carefully wiping their faces after eating.

QUENCHING JUNGLE THIRST

Slurp. Smack. Juicy fruits provide orangutans with almost all the liquid they need. As well, the orangutans catch rain with their tongues and lick drops of water off plant leaves or their own fur.

When fruit is scarce, orangutans look for water stored in vase-shaped plants or in holes in trees. They tip the plants up to drink, often swallowing floating insects as a bonus. And they make sponges by chewing leaves and use them to soak up water from the tree holes.

11

World in Motion

ORANGUTANS AREN'T JUMPERS OR LEAPERS. Still, they manage to get around the jungle just fine. Clambering with hands and feet, they move nimbly through tangles of branches and thick vines high above the ground.

But an orangutan also "pole-vaults" to get from one big tree to another. First, it str-e-t-ches out to grab a slender tree—its "pole"—then hops on. Moving back and forth, it starts the pole swaying, as you might pump a playground swing. The orangutan tugs on branches of nearby trees to aim the pole in the right direction. Then

Grabbing a vine, an orangutan swings through the forest.

the ape rides the swaying pole to the next large tree.

To move down a level in the jungle, an orangutan may take an "escalator." It uses the weight of its own body to bend a flexible tree, and then grabs onto the next tree.

If there's a dead tree—a snag—within reach, the orangutan grasps it with its hands and pushes off with its feet. When the snag snaps

An orangutan on the ground sometimes stands on two feet.

and falls, the orangutan rides down with it, clutching the branch of a live tree seconds before the snag crashes. Sometimes the great ape falls and breaks a bone or two.

How far orangutans travel depends on how easily they can find food. On some days, they go no more than 300 metres (about 1,000 feet). On other days, they might have to travel three times that distance. Full-grown males usually go the farthest. They must cover a lot of jungle to satisfy their huge appetites.

TRAVELING WAYS

Few orangutans spend much time walking—moving upright or shuffling along on all four fists. On land, they tend to be clumsy and slow. But among the trees, most orangutans travel as gracefully as trapeze artists.

In Sumatra, orangutans usually stay high up in the jungle, where they avoid attacks from hungry tigers on the prowl. However, in Borneo—where orangutans have few natural enemies—huge males go walking. Their heavy weight makes it hard to travel by tree.

World of Words

THROUGH THE JUNGLE COMES A LONG, LOUD CRY. An orangutan is calling. If it's looking for a mate, it might simply be saying, "I'm over here." But if it's a male trying to warn another male, the cry likely means, "Go away."

Both male and female adult orangutans have throat pouches that make their noisy calls louder. The sound can carry through the jungle for several kilometres (a few miles).

The throat pouch of a male is bigger than a female's. Dangling from the chin and throat, his pouch droops under his arms and passes over his shoulders. When the

Thick cheek pads aren't attractive, but they help a male orangutan deliver long-distance calls.

17

A young orangutan throws squeaky kisses through puckered lips.

orangutan cries out, he fills the loose skin with air. Then it deflates slowly as he broadcasts his calls.

Cheek pads on the faces of adult male orangutans make the sounds travel even farther. The thick growths direct their calls forward.

When two males meet, they usually

threaten each other. Besides bellowing and puffing up their throat pouches, they stare eye to eye. They might break off tree branches and shake them around. If that doesn't force one of the males to back off, the two might start fighting. They can battle to the death.

Male orangutans also have silent ways of delivering messages. By spreading their musky smells like love notes around the jungle, they encourage females to find them.

THROWING KISSES

Press your lips together and suck in air. The noise, called a "kiss-squeak," is an orangutan's way of saying that it's annoyed. Some orangutans vary the sound of their kiss-squeaks by covering their mouths with their hands or with leaves.

Now blow out hard and vibrate your tongue through your pressed lips. Scientists aren't sure exactly what that splattering noise—called a "raspberry"—means to orangutans. But for some, it's part of a going-to-bed routine.

New World

SNIFFING, LISTENING, LOOKING,
a female orangutan hunts through the
jungle for a mate. But she usually doesn't
need to search for too long—or too often.
During her lifetime of 35 to 40 years, she
reproduces only three or four times, first
giving birth as a young teen. Her babies
are born eight years apart.

At birth, an orangutan is small enough
to fit on the palm of your hand. It weighs
just half as much as a newborn human—but
it has a lot more hair.

An infant orangutan is well cared for.
Its mother feeds and guards it carefully. And

Brand new to
the world, a
tiny orangutan
cuddles close
to its mother.

she never sets the newborn down—not for a minute.

Still, a mother orangutan must have her arms free to climb from branch to branch and to travel from tree to tree. So the infant clings to her. Day and night, it clutches her fur in its four tiny fists or grabs whatever it can hang onto—sometimes her nose!

Hanging on, an infant orangutan grips its mother's fur tightly.

During its first year, the infant seems glued to its mother. Then bit by bit, it dares to move away, a few paces at a time. The infant travels with its mother while she eats, but it lives only on the warm milk from her body.

If the mother of an infant orangutan dies, another orangutan might adopt it. The new parent is usually a female adult who has lost an infant. The adoptive mother cares for the orangutan at least until she gives birth to an infant of her own.

HANDS OFF!

A ball of fluffy orange hair, a newborn orangutan squirmed in its mother's arms. She shifted the infant, letting it suckle her milk. Its teeny fingers tightened around long strands of her coat, and the infant dozed. So did the mother.

A zookeeper reached out to give the infant a gentle pat. And suddenly, the mother erupted with rage. She bared her fangs. Her hair stood on end. The message was clear: "Don't dare touch my baby!"

23

Small World

ORANGUTAN MOTHERS HAVE BIG JOBS. Next to human mothers, they spend more years caring for their young than any other animal in the world. Young orangutans take up to 12 years to learn all they must know to survive. As well, they depend heavily on their mothers' milk for four to seven years!

While orangutans are feeding strictly on milk, they grow quite slowly, usually weighing less than 25 kilograms (55 pounds). But when they start eating solid foods, their growth speeds up.

From their mothers, orangutans learn

An orangutan learns where to find food by following its mother.

25

what to eat and how to eat it. At first, the mothers prepare the food for their young, grinding it up with their teeth, then spitting it back out. Gradually, small orangutans learn to chew their own meals.

Finding enough of the right kinds of food in the dense jungle can be hard, so mother orangutans

When young orangutans meet, they enjoy playing with each other.

show their young where to look. The little ones learn which trees to target and the best times of the year to visit them.

As they grow up, the young orangutans start climbing on their own. Where it is hard to travel, a mother orangutan might grab hold of two trees at once and let her young one use her body as a bridge.

A daughter often stays with her mother longer than a son does. The daughter watches her mother raise another infant, learning how to care for her own family one day.

A young orangutan doesn't spend its whole day learning, eating, and napping. Like other intelligent animals, it likes to play. Grabbing hold of jungle vines, it swings from tree to tree—just for the fun of it. And it might hang upside down from a vine and splash itself with water.

When orangutans grow bigger, they like riding snags that snap and fall. Although snag-riding is a way to travel, it's also a sport that orangutans enjoy, especially when other orangutans are around.

27

Index